FLUEN'
ON THE FIRST TRY

HOW TO LEARN ANY LANGUAGE AND NEVER QUIT

FEDERICA LUPIS

Fluent on the first try
How to learn any language and never quit
By Federica Lupis

Disclaimer

The information in this book is true and complete to the best of the author's knowledge. While every attempt has been made to verify the information in this book, the author does not accept any responsibility for errors, inaccuracies or omissions.

This book is presented for informational purposes only. Any advice or recommendations are made without guarantee on the part of the author. The author disclaims any liability in connection with the use of the information contained in this book.

Mention of specific companies, organisations, authorities or websites does not imply endorsement by the author, nor does mention of specific companies, organisations, authorities or websites imply that they endorse this book or the author. The author mentioned specific companies, organisations, authorities or websites solely as a convenience to you.

First edition, December 2020
Editors: Ash Nandoskar and Michael Deves
Cover concept: Federica Lupis
Cover design: MiblArt

https://www.federicalupis.com/

To my family and friends
I love you with all my heart.

To all learners of foreign languages
Never give up. You will succeed.

Table of Contents

I'd love to hear from you!

Acknowledgements

About the author

Other books from the same author

Editorial work

INTRODUCTION

The story of how I became fluent is like that of many other learners.

I wasn't good at languages, and I didn't enjoy learning until one day I changed my learning method, and I improved. I even started to like languages; to the point that a few years later, I made a career out of them.

After becoming fluent in English, French and Spanish, I set my eyes on Japanese.

'As long as I use the same learning strategies, I'll be fine' I thought to myself, but it wasn't the case, and I repeatedly quit.

This time I had a different problem. If I knew what I had to do, why did I keep failing?

Starting all over again wasn't fun, but every time I quit, I learned something about the reasons why I couldn't achieve my goal.

I like to think that thanks to my experience, I can now help **you**!

In this book, you will discover how to learn any language you want and keep making progress until you become fluent.

Whether you are new to foreign languages or have some experience on your side, the advice in this book can make the difference between achieving your goal and forgetting about it.

With that said, let's do it!

IS THIS BOOK FOR YOU?

This book is for you if you:

~Are new to foreign languages and don't know how to go about learning.

~Have tried to learn a language but struggled to commit to it.

~Are learning a language but feel like you're not making progress.

I will walk you through the learning process from start to finish, making sure you understand how to reach your goal.

Tip For the best experience, I recommend reading this book in the order it is written. You can read these chapters in any order you like, but I think the suggested progression will give you the most benefit.

WHEN THIS BOOK IS NOT FOR YOU

Are you looking for the best strategies to learn the pronunciation, vocabulary and grammar of any language, and a detailed list of conversation exercises? In this case, my other book *Why you're not fluent and how to fix it*[1] is for you!

Fluent on the first try focuses on other aspects of the learning process.

Here you will find out how to:
~Make learning a language a habit.
~Avoid the risk of giving up halfway.
~Keep making progress until you become fluent (including practical examples of how you can improve your conversation skills).

---

[1] *Why you're not fluent and how to fix it* is available on all Amazon marketplaces in the e-book and paperback format. You can find the link to your Amazon marketplace on my website https://www.federicalupis.com/my-books.

Depending on your experience with languages, you may find one of my books more suitable to your needs or a combination of the two may give you the most benefit.

Together, my books reveal the key to becoming fluent:

~Use the learning strategies that work best for you. (*Why you're not fluent and how to fix it* guides the reader in selecting the most effective strategies for them.)

~Commit to learning and go beyond a solid knowledge of vocabulary and grammar. (*Fluent on the first try* will explain how you can make learning a language a habit and advance until you become fluent.)

When these two points are addressed, learners get amazing results.

CHAPTER ONE

FROM 'I WISH' TO 'LET'S DO IT!'

SAYING IT IS NOT ENOUGH

Six years ago, I decided it was time to do all the things I've always wanted to do but never did.

I wrote a long list of activities ranging from experimenting with new recipes to going for a swim once a week. Among my good resolutions, I included 'becoming fluent in Japanese'.

I thought that if I wrote it down, it would be like making a promise to myself. Unfortunately, I didn't commit to learning Japanese until several years later, and it wasn't thanks to my list. It was thanks to the strategies I am about to share with you.

As with anything else you want to achieve, saying that you want to learn a language is not enough to make it happen; you also need to act upon it. This book will show you how.

In Chapter One, you will discover how to make learning a language a habit and where to find the motivation to reach your goal. Chapter Two will reveal how you can keep learning and avoid the risk of giving up halfway. Finally, in Chapter Three, you will learn how to advance towards fluency, staying confident about your goal.

After reading this book, you'll have all the tools you need to make your wish of becoming fluent come true.

KNOW YOUR GOAL

Why are you learning a language? Is it for work, pleasure, or both? Your goal is important because it may be easier to quit if you don't know what you want.

To give you an example, one of my students decided to learn Italian[2] before her trip to Europe. She said she wanted to exchange some basic information while travelling and I organised our lessons accordingly.

We had just started our second month of classes when she suddenly dropped out.

I was surprised because I thought she was doing well, so I asked to meet her for coffee, hoping to find out more.

As we were chatting, my student said she got a call from an Italian friend: 'We tried to speak

---

[2] I was born in Italy, so my first language is Italian.

Italian, but I couldn't understand anything. We'd better speak English when I meet her this summer'.

An Italian friend? And she wanted to speak Italian with her?

'Is that why you don't want to continue our lessons?' I asked. 'Yes, I don't see the point. If I can't talk to my friend on the phone, I doubt it will be better in person.'

My student set an objective, but then assessed her results against a different goal.

Learning how to make conversation takes a lot more time and effort than remembering a few sentences; it also requires a completely different learning plan.

Without that conversation, my student would have dropped out for the wrong reasons. She wanted to quit because she didn't know what she wanted.

So now I want to ask you: why are you learning a foreign language?

Maybe you're doing it for fun, and you don't mind if it takes a long time to make progress. Maybe you're doing it for work, and you want to learn how to speak as soon as possible.

Whatever the reason, you should be clear about your goal **before** you start learning a language.

Knowing what you want will make it easier to choose which activities to do and assess your progress. It will also make it easier to reach your goal.

JUST DO IT

Before I could work as an interpreter in Australia, I had to pass a notoriously difficult exam. I wish I could tell you I faced the test bravely, but it was quite the opposite.

As soon as I realised that there were no interpreting courses in my area, I gave up.

I thought it was impossible to prepare for an exam on my own, so I didn't even try.

I'm not sure I'd work as an interpreter today if I hadn't come across Napoleon Hill's quote: 'Start where you stand, and work whatever tools you may have at your command and better tools will be found as you go along'.

His words changed everything. I started studying and passed the exam less than a year later.

In case you are wondering how this happened, the answer is: I just tried. I began to work towards what I wanted and realised I didn't need a degree to pass the exam. I could do it alone!

Sometimes the hardest part of achieving our goals is to start. The fear of failing or choosing the wrong path can hold us back and become an obstacle to what we want.

As a learner of foreign languages, you may question your choices at any point in the learning process. You may wonder if you are using the best resources and methods; even if you have what it takes to reach your goal.

The best way not to get stuck is to take action, regardless of any doubts you may have.

For example, if you're undecided between podcasts and apps to learn grammar, try both and see how it goes. This is the only way to find out what works best for you.

If you keep waiting until you get the best resources or the perfect method, you may never start. So just do it! The rest will fall into place as you go along.

HOW LONG WILL IT TAKE?

Most learners wonder how long it will take to become fluent. It is a legitimate question. When you put in the effort to do something, you want to know when you can see the results.

The truth is, it is difficult for someone else to give you an answer.

The experience of other learners can give you a rough idea, but your progress will depend on **what you do** to reach your goal.

How often do you actually spend time on the foreign language? Do you do different activities? Are you practising conversation? You are the only person who knows the answers to these questions.

By considering both the results of other learners and your approach to learning, you'll be able to set a realistic time frame and avoid unreasonable expectations.

Too many learners give up on a language when their results don't match someone else's. I don't want you to do the same.

If you talk to someone who has become fluent, make sure to ask them lots of questions. What kind of activities did they do? How often? Do they know other foreign languages?

If you just focus on the time it took them to reach their goal, you'll end up having unrealistic expectations.

It's pointless to compare your results to someone else's without considering all relevant factors.

For example, I think I could become fluent in Portuguese in a couple of months. My claim might seem incredible if I didn't add any details to it.

Now let me tell you the whole story.

For me, Portuguese is like a mixture of Italian, Latin and Spanish. I am a native Italian speaker, I have a good knowledge of Latin, and I am fluent in Spanish. This is why I can already read Portuguese, a language I have never studied before.

I also forgot to mention that my goal would be achievable if learning Portuguese was all I do. I wouldn't have time for work and many other things.

By now, my claim should no longer seem sensational…

As a learner, it is exciting to think about when you'll be fluent. Understanding your favourite movie or having a full conversation in a foreign language will be an unforgettable experience.

The essential thing is that time doesn't turn into a make-or-break factor. You can set a deadline and work towards it, but you should be ready to make adjustments to your prediction as you go.

There are so many factors that influence the learning process that it is crucial to have some flexibility.

Tip To get a better idea of how long it might take to become fluent, you can check the Foreign Service Institute's learning timelines.[3] Their findings are based on seventy years of

---

[3] You can find the results of their study online at the address: https://www.state.gov/foreign-language-training/.

experience in teaching languages to U.S. diplomats.

In short, the Foreign Service Institute (FSI) divided over sixty languages into four categories, depending on the level of difficulty. For each group, they specified how many class hours/weeks it should take to achieve proficiency (for example, approximately 600/750 class hours for Portuguese, 1100 class hours for Russian, and 2200 class hours for Mandarin).

As the FSI points out, timelines are based on 'the average length of time' for a student to become proficient. Results may vary depending on other factors such as the knowledge of other foreign languages.

In any case, the FSI's data provide some useful guidelines on how long it may take to master a language.

Note If the language you are learning isn't mentioned on the FSI's website, you can start a discussion on a language forum where other learners can share their experience with you.[4]

ABOUT SHORTCUTS

The first time I tried to learn Japanese, I decided it would happen quickly.

I had heard of so many shortcuts and success stories! I was sure one of them would work for me too.

After browsing the Internet, I found a book that promised to make me fluent in Japanese in five minutes a day, in a matter of months. I bought it without thinking twice…

---

[4] To find a language forum for your language of interest, search on the Internet: 'language+language forum', e.g. 'Hindi language forum'.

For the first week, I felt hopeful and motivated. I repeated words that I couldn't even read, but I believed everything would soon make sense.

Halfway through the second week, doubt crept into my thoughts. Had I taken the bait of false promises? No, I was too smart for that.

Week three was the week of denial; until I got to the end of week four. I had just studied Japanese for a month and couldn't even count to ten. What was going on?

I soon realised that I was wasting my time.

Instead of blaming the book, I started doubting myself. Maybe I wasn't good enough to learn a language on my own.

I was so disappointed that I decided to take a break and return to Japanese soon. Unfortunately, that break turned into years.

The book wasn't the only culprit, but it played a big part in my decision to stop learning. With better resources, I would have had more chances of success.

When learning a language, quick learning methods are always tempting, but it's better not to trust them blindly like I did.

More often than not, these are just marketing strategies promising the impossible to sell their products. The problem is that they give you false confidence that you can do it, and when they don't work, you may think it's your fault, when in fact it was a lie to sell something from the start.

If you don't want to waste your time, you should do a little research before you use any shortcut. Can you talk to other learners who have used it? Did it work as promised?

When something sounds too good to be true, it probably is!

The good news is, you don't need shortcuts. As you are about to find out, you just need the right motivation and a little planning.

PLAN AHEAD

The last time I tried to learn Japanese (and failed), I was working and writing a book. To keep costs down, I decided to study on my own. I knew it would take me longer than if I had a teacher, but I was willing to make an effort.

At the time, I had already become fluent in three languages. And I thought that as long as I chose a good book, I could reach my goal.

Little did I know that the learning material would be the least of my problems.

This time I had everything I needed to get started, but I never did. Every day something came up, or there was something more important to do.

First, there was work and my book, then I had to clean the house and so on and so forth. In the meantime, my Japanese book was 'swallowed' by a pile of papers that were obviously more urgent than learning a language.

Six months went by, and I forgot about my exciting plan to read comics in Japanese. Until one day a friend asked me: 'How's the studying going?'

Japanese?! I didn't even remember that I wanted to learn it! How did she remember my goal?

That day I decided that I would find the time to learn. Alas, I couldn't make days longer, but I could definitely take a better look at my schedule and rearrange a few things.

What I did was pretty simple: I made a list of my daily tasks (including time and place) and highlighted the free time slots. There weren't many, but at least there were some.

Then I chose three hours per week to learn Japanese and set a reminder on my phone. At first, having a plan wasn't enough; I needed some encouragement to commit to it.

This strategy helped me find some time to learn a language. But above all, it made me realise that my goal was achievable, and I felt more confident that I could do it.

If you feel like your schedule is too tight, or always end up doing something else, you should try this strategy. It will help you find some time to learn and make a habit of it.

Just remember that some days may be better than others to practise your language skills. For example, an hour of study after working, cleaning the house, and making dinner may not be as good as an hour of study on Sunday morning after getting some sleep.

By giving more structure to the learning process, you will realise that you have time for a language even if you have other important things to do.

With a little planning, learning will become one of your priorities, and there will be no room for procrastination.

Tip If no matter how you look at your schedule, it seems too tight to learn a language, perhaps you can reorganise some of your daily activities. Can you spend less time on any of them to 'buy' some time for learning? And even better, can you combine different tasks?

For example, if you do a crossword every morning, would you be willing to do it in a foreign language? How about listening to music in a foreign language while cleaning the house?

These are just some examples of how you can incorporate a language into your already planned activities. Can you come up with more ideas? So you can keep learning without needing to find more time.

Note Time management apps like *Rescue Time*[5] can make your task easier.

THE ALTERNATIVE

A friend of mine once asked me for advice on how to learn a language. She said planning was not her style: 'It stresses me out. I have to do so many things on a schedule. If learning a

---

[5] https://www.rescuetime.com/

language is one of them, it will become a task, and I will lose interest. What can I do if I don't want to plan?'

'Nothing', I said. 'You will never learn a language.'

The look on her face was priceless. She thought I was serious, but eventually, she realised I was just making fun of her.

My friend made a good point. Not everyone can plan their weeks in advance, and even if they could, it might take the fun out of learning. So what's the alternative?

You can start with ten minutes a day. Maybe you can listen to a podcast on the way to work? Use an app during your lunch break? Read a book in the foreign language before bed? It doesn't matter which activity you choose, as long as you do it regularly.

Some of you may argue that ten minutes isn't enough to learn, but that's not the point.

The idea is to help you make learning a language a habit without having to organise too much in advance. Once it becomes part of your routine, you may end up working on it longer than expected.

A short time commitment will make it harder to fail. By reaching your goal, again and again, you will be encouraged to do more, and learning a language will become more spontaneous.

I know because I did it with exercise. Planning sessions wasn't working for me. There was always something coming up, and I kept putting it off.

Then I tried this strategy, and my attitude changed. I realised that I was making any excuse not to exercise because I felt like it was a chore and I didn't want to do it.

If planning isn't your style, try this strategy. It may be just what you need.

MAKE THE MOST OF YOUR TIME

Since I moved to Australia, I have become increasingly attached to my phone. My family and lifelong friends are in Italy, and sharing messages and photos with them makes me feel closer to home.

I used to keep my phone by my side all the time; including when I was learning Japanese. As soon as a notification popped up, I checked it. If my phone rang, I dropped everything to answer it.

After a couple of weeks, I realised that I wasn't learning as much as I expected and I couldn't understand why. It didn't even occur to me that the phone was distracting me and making it harder for me to learn.

Luckily, once I made the connection, my study time became a 'phone-free zone', and I started learning faster.

My experience has helped me understand that motivation and planning become irrelevant if you don't get rid of distractions first. This applies to languages and anything else you want to achieve.

Maybe you're already one step ahead of me, and you know that learning and messaging don't go well together. Either way, taking a second to consider if something is distracting you won't hurt.

For example, is your neighbour listening to Eminem at full volume while you are learning a language? Your neighbour has excellent taste, but you can't listen to music just now; put some earplugs on.

Are there people coming and going where you are studying? It's probably best if you move to a quieter place like your local library or park.

Distractions can slow down your progress. That's why you should get rid of them.

Give your full attention to what you are doing, and you will learn much more in a shorter period of time.

ABOUT MULTITASKING

Some people are great at multitasking. I have a friend who can type while talking on the phone and doing her nails. (No kidding; I've seen it happen!)

If you enjoy doing different things at once, this strategy can help you make more time for learning. The essential thing is to choose activities that work well together.

For example, I had a student who listened to an Italian podcast while exercising. Lifting weights didn't take her attention off the lessons, and her language skills significantly improved.

I also had a friend who was trying to learn Spanish while cooking. Dolores (fake name) used to watch movies with subtitles as she was slicing vegetables in the kitchen. Luckily, she wasn't learning much and decided to quit.

Multitasking can help you maximise your time, but it can also make you waste it.

Apart from avoiding dangerous choices (think slicing vegetables while looking at a screen), consider how much you would learn while doing different things.

For example, would it be useful to listen to the news in the foreign language as you are doing the dishes? Unless you're wearing headphones, you may not hear much.

If you want to multitask, choose activities that work well together. This way, you will devote quality time to learning and get the most out of your efforts.

KNOW WHEN IT'S ENOUGH

It took me six months to write my university thesis. Considering I was working and studying, while taking care of my social life, it was a reasonable amount of time. However, if I could go back in time and give myself some advice, it would be to work less on it.

I don't mean that I should have neglected my thesis; I simply should have managed my time better.

To give you an example, if I had the afternoon off, I would spend it all writing. This may sound great, but it wasn't.

After several hours, I got tired. Making sense of what I had in mind became harder, and the quality of my writing was anything but stellar. Because of this, I had to spend more time editing or rewriting entire sections.

I am convinced that if I had stopped writing when my mind got clouded, I would have finished my thesis much earlier.

Thanks to my experience, I realised that spending more time on something doesn't necessarily mean better results. This is as true for writing as it is for learning a language.

You can study for one hour at a time and be more productive than if you study for three hours straight.

I see it with Japanese. I do more in one hour because I am more focused. Working under a time constraint has helped me become more efficient, and my productivity has increased.

When you're learning a language, you shouldn't put too much weight on the amount of time. Instead, you should ask yourself: 'Can I still concentrate? Can I pay full attention to what I'm doing?'

If the answer is no, it means you've done enough. You can go back to learning later or another day.

Your mind needs a break. If you go past your attention span, you won't achieve much. On the contrary, you may stress yourself out and be tempted to give up on learning.

HOW TO FIND YOUR MOTIVATION

There was one thing I used to hate more than pineapple on pizza, and that was flossing.

When I brushed my teeth, it was late, and I was half asleep. Flossing required time and effort, and most of the time, it would wake me up, so I just did it once in a while and thought it would be okay.

This was before my dentist presented me with a seven-hundred-dollar bill to fix two teeth. I was shocked and deeply regretted my decision to ignore his past warnings.

This time, I was going to floss every night, and I was going to stick to it; but how? I needed the motivation to do it, and I knew I would soon forget my hefty bill. So I printed it out and put it in my drawer on top of my pyjamas.

Every night, I would open my drawer to get ready for bed, and that bill would be there to remind me of the consequences of not flossing.

It was an extreme measure, but for someone whose teeth used to decay easily, it worked wonders. After a couple of months, I threw the bill away, and I am still flossing every night, no matter how late it is.

With my story, I am not trying to convince you to floss or suggest that you put a warning sign to learn a language on your breakfast placemat. I want to stress the importance of finding the motivation to do things.

What can motivate you to learn a language? It may be easy to start, but how do you keep going?

Here are some ideas for you:

~**Use what you love**. You can use most of your passions as an incentive to learn a language. For example, one of my students regularly watches soccer matches in Italian, while another hasn't missed an episode of *Money Heist* in Spanish.

What do you like doing in your free time? Singing? Playing video games? Reading horror stories?

Finding the motivation to learn a language may be as easy as choosing a song, game, or book in a foreign language.

~Tell people. A friend of mine took to social media to announce that he would learn Russian and Spanish.

At first, I thought that telling everyone about his goal was a bit rushed. He had never learned a language before, and now he wanted to learn two. What if he changed his mind?

Then I realised it was a smart move.

When my friend says he will do something, he will go above and beyond to keep his word. That's why he told everyone about his goal.

If this sounds like you, start spreading the word about your desire to learn a language. You may work harder because you don't want to let anyone down.

~Team up. There was no love lost between me and biology in high school. Yet, I didn't mind getting ready for a test, as I was always studying with my best friend, Vanessa.

Learning a foreign language doesn't have to be a solo experience. If you like the idea of studying with someone, don't think twice: find a friend who wants to join you!

By sharing this experience, you may be more committed to your goal and excited about learning.

Suddenly, it wouldn't be 'you against the language'; you would have 'a partner in crime' to support you.

When you can't understand something, you can discuss it and look for solutions together. When you feel like throwing your book against the wall, you can laugh about it and quickly shake it off.

In my experience, studying with a friend will give you more motivation to work towards your goal.

Tip As an alternative to studying with a friend, you can join a language club in your area.

For those who are not familiar with this concept, language clubs are groups of people who meet regularly to practise their language skills.

There are groups for beginners, so you don't need to worry if you only have a basic knowledge of the language.

All you need is a genuine interest in learning and making friends.

To find language clubs in your area, visit *Meetup*[6] or *Polyglot Club*.[7]

~Get a teacher. Some learners need a teacher. Not because they wouldn't be able to learn on their own, but because their teacher becomes their source of motivation.

To give you an example, in secondary school, I thought I had zero chances of learning how to draw, but my teacher was so motivating that I did my best to improve. As a result, I did well in what appeared to be an impossible task.

---

[6] https://www.meetup.com/
[7] https://polyglotclub.com/

I believe the same can happen to anyone who wants to learn a language.

Do you do more when you are encouraged and praised for your efforts? In this case, finding your motivation may be as simple as getting a teacher.

Teachers have been learners themselves, so they know how to best support you and guide you towards your goal.

~Keep track of your hard work. We should do so many things to stay healthy that I feel dizzy just thinking about it. Eating superfoods, sleeping eight hours, meditating, exercising... It's only the tip of the iceberg when it comes to living a healthy life.

I want to be healthy. Who doesn't? But honestly, I got to a point where I didn't know what else to do to find some time to exercise.

Waking up at 6 am was out of the question –
then I wouldn't get my eight hours of sleep!
Maybe I could exercise while I was eating?!

As usual, I just had to take a deep breath and
have a better look at my schedule.

I started exercising ten minutes a day, no
matter what. I apologise to those who regularly
go to the gym, but for me, it was a big
commitment.

Now that I had found the time, how could I
motivate myself to keep doing it?

I used a calendar. I hung it up in the kitchen
and wrote the word 'gym' in capital letters every
time I exercised.

It made me feel so good! As I cooked, I could
appreciate my efforts.

My calendar worked so well that I did the same
for Japanese. Seeing how many language

activities I do week after week motivates me to do more.

Could a calendar do the same for you?

~**Look at other learners**. After reading a few pages of this book, you know I wasn't good at foreign languages and struggled to commit to Japanese.

I am now fluent in four languages, and I am learning a fifth.

Doesn't that make you feel like you can become fluent too?

It should!

Very few people are born with a gift for languages. Most learners had to try and fail before they found their way to success.

Reading other learners' stories and realising that most have had setbacks can give you more confidence that you can do it too!

~Get inspired. When I began to write my university thesis, I noticed that a sudden fear of the unknown was taking over.

I immediately started looking for a job, but the salary I was offered as a soon-to-be graduate was barely enough to cover rent and groceries. At the time, I was working as a sales assistant and earning more money than the jobs I was applying for in my field of study.

Should I have kept my current job? Or accepted the underpaid one and hoped the pay would rise soon enough?

Looking back, I know I shouldn't have worried about it, but back then, I felt like my decision would change the course of my life.

Then one day, a friend of mine suggested that I watch Steve Jobs' commencement address to the graduates of Stanford University.[8]

Not only did I stop looking for a job, but I also decided to move to London and try my luck.

Motivational quotes and speeches can be powerful. They can show us things from a different perspective and inspire us to work towards our goal.

If you are looking for a boost of motivation, you can't go wrong with them.

~Test your skills. Are you result driven? Do you do your best when you have a deadline? Then taking a proficiency exam might be the best option for you.

---

[8] To watch Steve Jobs' speech, search on YouTube: 'Steve Jobs' commencement address to the graduates of Stanford University'.

Some learners become more focused as soon as they decide to get a formal assessment of their language skills.

If this sounds like you, check out Wikipedia's 'list of proficiency tests by language'[9] or search the Internet[10] for more options.

Booking your exam may increase your desire to learn.

~**Travel abroad**. In 2018, my dream of visiting Egypt finally came true. I've always had a passion for Ancient Egypt, and the chance to see the Great Pyramid of Giza, Luxor and the Abu Simbel temples warmed my heart.

There is only one thing that could have made my trip even more memorable, and that is being able to read Egyptian hieroglyphs. If I go

---

[9] https://en.wikipedia.org/wiki/List_of_language_proficiency_tests
[10] To find a list of proficiency tests, search on the Internet: 'your language + proficiency tests', e.g. 'Polish proficiency tests'.

back someday, I'd like to learn them to be able to immerse myself in Ancient Egypt's culture.

Next time you get the chance to plan a trip abroad, consider a place where you can use the foreign language; it will be a great incentive to learn more.

~**Do some brainstorming**. This was just a quick list of ideas to find more motivation to learn a language. Now you can do some brainstorming and come up with more.

Think about something you've achieved in the past. Can you use the same motivation to learn a language?

If you have no clue, ask your family and friends. People who know you well may give you good advice on what drives you to do things.

A SIMPLE PLAN

As a child, I felt like it was much easier to do things. If I wanted to take a bike ride, I didn't have to plan ahead. Once my homework was done, I was free to go. Now, before I even go for a walk, I need to consider several tedious tasks.

It's normal. The more we grow up, the more responsibilities we have and even simple things can become hard to achieve.

Mastering a new language isn't usually part of our essential duties. This is why it can be difficult to commit to it.

The purpose of this first chapter was to help you give more structure to the learning process so that it's easier to fit it into your routine.

By now, you should have your objective clear in your mind; including how long it should take to reach it. All that's left to do is put together a plan. Don't worry, it only needs to be a simple one!

Grab a sheet of paper and write or start a new document and type:

~Your goal. Why are you learning a new language? Is it for fun? To travel? For work? Your goal is important because it may be easier to quit if you don't know what you want.

~A time frame. How long will it take to reach your goal? By considering both the results of other learners and your approach to learning, you'll be able to set a realistic time frame and avoid unreasonable expectations.

~Days and times of practice. Whether it's an hour every Sunday or ten minutes a day, you need to be specific. Will you practise at 3 pm or ten minutes during your lunch break? Otherwise, you may end up watching your favourite TV series or laughing at funny cat videos on social media (at least that's what I would do).

~List of your preferred learning activities. Deciding what to do during your learning sessions can take time. A short list of your preferred pronunciation, grammar, vocabulary and conversation activities will help you choose faster. It will also be a good reminder to do different things.

If all you do to learn a language is complete grammar exercises, you may become the Incredible Hulk of grammar, but it will be hard to excel at conversation.

~How you will periodically assess your progress. A good plan not only includes what you want and how you want to achieve it, but it also tells you how you will assess your results. For example, to get feedback on your progress, you could take a language proficiency test or book monthly sessions with a tutor. Otherwise, it will be difficult to know if you are on the right track.

And that's all you should include in your plan. Once it's ready, make sure it's easy to access when you're studying.

For example, you could keep a copy of your plan on your desk, one on your phone, and one on your computer desktop. If you hang it in the laundry where you transit once a week, it might smell like 'summer breeze', but it won't help much.

Putting a plan together shouldn't take long, and your time will be well invested. It will give you a clear vision of what you want and how you want to achieve it, and help you commit to learning a language more.

ACTION PLAN

~Define your goal.

~Set a realistic time frame.

~Find your motivation.

~Plan your learning sessions (whether it is ten minutes a day or twice a week).

~Start working towards what you want.

~Make a list of your preferred learning activities.

~Use shortcuts and multitasking only when appropriate and effective.

~Get rid of distractions.

~Take a break when you need it.

~Periodically assess your results.

~Ignore doubts and keep going! You learn by doing, not waiting.

CHECKPOINT

~You have a plan and the motivation to reach your goal ✔

Well done! You're ready for the next step!

RECAP

~Why are you learning a foreign language? Is it for work, pleasure, or both? Your goal is important because it may be easier to quit if you don't know what you want.

~Sometimes the hardest part of achieving our goal is to start. As a learner of foreign languages, you may question your choices at any point in the learning process. The best way not to get stuck is to take action, regardless of any doubts you may have.

~How long will it take to become fluent? By considering both the results of other learners and your approach to learning, you'll be able to set a realistic time frame and avoid unreasonable expectations.

~If you want to use a shortcut, you should do some research first. Can you talk to other learners who have used it? Did it work as promised? When a shortcut seems too good to be true, it probably is.

~Plan your learning sessions. Take a look at your schedule and make a list of your daily tasks. Then decide when you can dedicate time to a language and set a reminder on your phone. With a little planning, learning a language will become one of your priorities, and there will be no room for procrastination.

~If planning is not your style, commit to learning a language ten minutes a day. A short time commitment will make it harder to fail. By reaching your goal, again and again, you will feel encouraged to do more, and learning a language will turn into a habit.

~Distractions can slow down your progress. That's why you should get rid of them. Give your full attention to what you are doing, and you will learn much more in a shorter period of time.

~If you want to make more time for learning, multitasking is an excellent idea, but you should choose activities that work well together. This way, you will devote quality time to learning and get the most out of your efforts.

~Take a break when you need it. You can study for one hour at a time and be more productive than if you study for three hours straight.

~What can motivate you to learn a language? It may be easy to start, but how do you keep going? If you have no clue, ask your family and friends. People who know you well may give you good advice on what drives you to do things.

~Put together a simple plan and make sure it's easy to access when you're studying. Being reminded of what you want and how you want to achieve it will help you commit to learning a language more.

CHAPTER TWO

HOW TO KEEP GOING

Finding the motivation to learn a language, and acting upon it, is half the battle. Once a language is part of your routine, it will be harder to quit, but not impossible. Other factors can take you away from your goal in the long term.

In this chapter, we will explore how you can keep learning and avoid the risk of giving up halfway.

STEP BY STEP

When I decided to learn Japanese, I knew I had to master around 2,000 characters[11] to be able to read fluently. I was a bit intimidated, but I was confident I could do it.

---

[11] Japanese characters are called kanji.

At some point, though, I realised that most characters had at least two pronunciations, and I felt overwhelmed. I thought learning everything would take forever.

If I didn't want to give up, I needed to make my goal more approachable, so I decided to break it into smaller ones.

'Two thousand characters' became 'ten characters a day'; a number that looked much more feasible.

As soon as I turned my attention to what I could do in one day, I felt relieved. What seemed like an insurmountable obstacle was now a path I could cross.

One of the most common reasons learners quit halfway is that they feel overwhelmed.

Learning a language means dealing with a significant amount of information. And if you measure your progress against your ultimate goal, it may be hard to advance.

The solution is to break your big goals into smaller ones.

For example, if you wanted to learn the 1,000 most used words in a foreign language, you could set a goal of 10 words per day and get it done in about three months. This would help you see your objective as something you can do at your own pace, without having to worry about how many words are left to learn.

Big goals may seem out of reach and intimidating, while small ones can give you more confidence that you can do it.

By taking it one step at a time, you won't feel overwhelmed, and it will be easier to keep learning.

ABOUT YOUR LEARNING STRATEGIES

One afternoon after school, I wanted to watch a movie with my sister Valentina, but she had to study for an English test.

The test involved writing a business letter, and she had to learn a long list of words. 'It will take me forever', she said. 'I don't think I'll have time today.'

I really wanted to watch *Gremlins* together, so I offered to help.

Valentina tried to memorise the English words by repeating them out loud. After five minutes, I tested her, but those words didn't seem to have stuck in her memory.

'Why don't you think about something you already know?' I suggested. 'For example, the word *sender* is similar to the surname of Steve Sanders from *Beverly Hills 90210*.'[12]

My sister learned the word *sender* right away, so we decided to make similar associations for the rest of the words on her list. An hour later, she was ready for the test, and we were able to watch the movie together. I couldn't have been happier!

At first, my sister tried to learn new words by reading them out loud, but it didn't work. It was only when she started using a better approach that she learned faster, and remembering new vocabulary became easier for her.

When learning a language, if you use the wrong strategies, it could take twice as long to learn. You may even start doubting yourself, to the point of giving up on your goal.

---

[12] A popular TV series in the nineties.

The only way around this is to try different strategies and find out what works best for you.

For example, to learn the grammar of a foreign language, you could try traditional exercises, podcasts and apps. You shouldn't just settle for the most popular method.

This approach will help you save time. Once you start using the most effective strategies, you will learn faster, and it will be easier to remember what you have learned.

You can find the best strategies to learn the pronunciation, vocabulary, grammar of any language, and a detailed list of conversation exercises, in my book *Why you're not fluent and how to fix it*.[13] There, I discuss traditional and innovative techniques in detail and help

---

[13] *Why you're not fluent and how to fix it* is available on all Amazon marketplaces in the e-book and paperback format. You can find the link to your Amazon marketplace on my website https://www.federicalupis.com/my-books.

the reader choose the ones that work best for them.

Alternatively, you can search on the Internet: *'Best strategies to learn + your language of interest (e.g. Russian) + pronunciation / grammar / vocabulary / conversation'.* Several blogs and forums give good advice on how to learn specific languages.

Either way, never settle for the first method you come across. Always look for the learning strategies that will help you learn in half the time and remember things in the long term.

QUESTION YOUR METHOD

My relationship with foreign languages started out as complicated.

I didn't like languages. I thought they were useless, and I often wondered why we didn't all speak the same one.

In my defence, my first contact with foreign languages was in secondary school. And I suspect my poor results had something to do with my ridiculous opinion.

I was convinced I could treat languages like any other subject.

My learning approach worked with everything, so it should have worked with foreign languages. If I didn't do well, the languages were to blame, not my perfect method!

Then one day, I had a revelation in the most unexpected way.

I decided to prepare for an English test with one of my classmates. I used to study alone, thinking I would be more productive, but I got to the point where I felt nothing could make me worse at languages than I already was.

As I opened my book, getting ready for my new battle, I repeated out loud the grammar rules I had memorised beforehand.

My friend looked at me as if I was speaking gibberish: 'What are you talking about? I thought we were studying English', she laughed.

That day, I realised that memorising rules was preventing me from learning. With the help of my friend, I started to focus on examples rather than definitions and, little by little, I made progress. I also began to like languages; to the point that a few years later, I made a career out of them.

If you are reading this book, chances are you already like languages. In any case, there is an invaluable lesson we can take from my younger self. That is to stop assuming that whatever we are doing to learn a language is the best option we have – especially when we are struggling to make progress.

Whether you are new to foreign languages or have some experience on your side, get ready to question your method. If I hadn't questioned mine, I would still be campaigning for 'one language for all'!

SET YOURSELF UP FOR SUCCESS

Imagine you've just bought a brush that promises to scrub your dishes in no time. When you get home, you can't wait to try it out, but as you start using it, you notice it's not very effective.

Would you keep using it? Probably not. Would you replace it with something else? Most likely.

Now apply the same idea to learning a language. Would you continue to use a book, website, or app that doesn't work as promised? Probably not. Would you replace it with something else? Maybe.

Why are you more likely to replace a dish brush than some learning resources?

On the one hand, it's for practical reasons. You have to clean the dishes, but usually, you don't need to learn a language. On the other, it's because of what you think when these two products don't work.

If a dish brush wasn't effective, you wouldn't blame yourself; you would probably dismiss it as a bad product. On the contrary, if some learning resources don't work as promised, you may blame yourself. You may start thinking that you are not good at languages and stop learning.

Choosing the appropriate learning material is as important as selecting the strategies that work best for you. This is why you should take the time to research your options.

Whether you are looking for a book, website or app, you should start from the Internet. There is no other place where you can compare the opinion of millions of learners on the best resources to use. It will be sufficient to type: 'best apps to learn Spanish', for example, and you will have access to thousands of reviews.

To avoid getting lost in an ocean of information, you can focus on the first page of results. If the same material is mentioned on different websites, that's a good sign.

The idea is to write a short list of resources that you would like to try so that you can choose which ones to use.

For better results, you can narrow down your search to the past year, in your search engine settings. I do this every time I'm looking for something, from technology to language resources. This way, I never miss out on the latest products.

Some learners prefer to skip this step and settle for the most popular resources. I think this choice is risky because you may end up using learning material that is not suitable for you.

Both as a learner and as a teacher, I found that some of the most sought-after resources were as bad as 'soy sauce on ice-cream' – it's a thing. I promise I didn't make it up! They were probably great for other learners, but after reading reviews and trying them out, I realised they were definitely not for me.

If you want to speed up the learning process, do a little research and try different things: the best learning material for you will help you improve your language skills much faster.

Tip If you are new to learning languages, or find the idea of searching the Internet overwhelming, you can start from *FluentU*,[14] *Fluent in 3 months*[15] and *Reddit*.[16] I find these websites very useful when it comes to tips on learning resources.

WITH NO DOUBTS

We cannot compare ourselves to the learners of the past.

Nowadays, we can learn anything we want from the comfort of our homes. All we have to do is access the Internet, and our questions will be answered.

Even if we are lucky, we don't always use this precious resource to its full potential. We often

---

[14] https://www.fluentu.com/en/
[15] https://www.fluentin3months.com/
[16] https://www.reddit.com/

forget that the Internet is not only the place where we can find the resources to learn a language. It's also a network where we can get the help and support of other learners.

There will be times when, no matter how hard you try, you won't be able to find the answer to your question on your own. For example, you may struggle to find a good explanation of how to use a word or grammar rule.

Instead of giving up on your question, you should post it on a language forum or discussion website (like *WordReference*,[17] *Quora*[18] and *Reddit*[19]) where other learners and native speakers can help.

This way, you will be able to compare different explanations and examples in the same place.

---

[17] https://www.wordreference.com/
[18] https://www.quora.com/
[19] https://www.reddit.com/

You will also have the opportunity to ask further questions until you solve your problem.

If you don't clarify your doubts, you may get to the point where you have so many that you feel overwhelmed.

By turning to the Internet and connecting with other people, you will make sure your questions don't build up, and you can stay focused on your goal.

This approach will make your learning experience more enjoyable. It's nice to know that if you get lost along the way, there is a place where you can easily get the help you need.

FORGET ABOUT IT

Some learners are so worried about learning grammar and vocabulary to perfection that they disregard any other activity. 'How can I watch a movie in a foreign language, if I haven't finished my grammar book yet?'

This kind of reasoning doesn't make much sense.

How will you know when you have learned enough words and rules? When will you be ready for other activities?

In any case, it is highly unlikely that you can learn all the words of a foreign language; maybe not even all the grammar rules.

Think of technical vocabulary, slang, and dialects, and you will realise that it is practically impossible to know every single word of a language. Pay attention to conversations in your language, and you will find that many native speakers don't follow all the grammar rules.

Then why would you aim at learning them to perfection?

I don't mean that you should neglect these aspects of a language; they are important. But you should loosen your grip on them; especially in the first stages of learning.

A basic knowledge of vocabulary and grammar is enough to be able to read, watch a movie, speak and do many other things.

By doing different activities, you will discover alternative ways of learning and make progress faster.

Don't let the idea of 'not knowing enough' slow you down.

ONE MORE REASON TO MIX THINGS UP

How would you feel if you could only eat pizza for a week? I love pizza, but I'm sure after a couple of days, I'd start craving a different meal.

The thing I love most about food is the variety. There are so many ingredients that I feel like the number of dishes I can create is infinite.

Limiting myself to the same meal would bore me to tears, and I would probably never want to taste it again.

I see the process of learning a language in a similar way.

As a learner, you should do different activities not to make the learning process repetitive.

If you always do the same things (for example, if you only do grammar exercises but never read a book or watch a movie), you may get so bored that you decide to quit.

On the contrary, if you do different activities, you will keep the learning process exciting and stimulating, and you will be more likely to succeed.

When I started studying Japanese, I tried to learn how to write first and then the rest, but I soon realised it wouldn't work. That kind of approach was very heavy.

As soon as I combined writing with grammar and included listening and speaking activities, I started to put in a lot more effort. And learning Japanese just got a lot more enjoyable.

If I had to choose one of the secrets to becoming fluent in a language, it would be the choice to do different activities. This is a great incentive to keep the interest high and continue learning.

SOMETHING YOU DON'T WANT TO DO WITHOUT

It is much harder to abandon activities that add value to the quality of our life. Ask someone who meditates or goes to the gym every day, and they will tell you that if they don't, they feel like something is missing.

To make sure you continue learning, you should make a language an important part of your life. This will help you perceive it as 'something you don't want to do without'.

You can start with small things, like changing your phone's language settings or listening to music in a foreign language. This is a simple way of fitting a language into your routine.

Then think about your hobbies and passions. Is there a way to use a language in relation to them? For example, suppose you are into fashion or cars. In that case, you could watch

YouTube videos on these topics in the foreign language.

Take some time to think about it, and I'm sure you'll find a way to use what you love as an incentive to learn.

Finally, consider volunteering or joining a language club. You could use the language you are learning to help someone in your community or share your experience with other learners to improve your skills.[20]

One of the most significant drop-out factors for learners is that they perceive a language as something they have to go to great lengths to learn.

If you can fit a language into your routine and make it an important aspect of your life, you will have a better chance of reaching your goal.

---

[20] For language clubs in your area, visit *Meetup* and *Polyglot Club*.

GET OUT OF YOUR COMFORT ZONE

Some people stop learning a language because they aren't making progress as fast as they expected.

They generally blame a lack of time and memory. However, spending more time on something doesn't necessarily mean you'll get better results, and memory has nothing to do with your talent for languages. It's your learning method that makes all the difference.

So far, we have discussed different ways to make progress in a language. If you have already put these strategies into practice, well done! You are on the right track.

There is just one more thing you need to add to your list. That is to say, you must be willing to get out of your comfort zone.

For example, if you want to improve your conversation skills, you should face a conversation challenge every week.

You could start by recording yourself as you say some simple sentences in the foreign language, then listen to your recording. Believe it or not, many people struggle with speaking because they are not used to hearing their voice in another language.

The next step could be to record yourself role-playing a conversation between two people. For example, think about checking in at a hotel. What would the receptionist ask you? How would you answer?

After practising on your own, you should organise a conversation session with a fluent or native speaker and use a dictionary to take some pressure off yourself.

It doesn't matter if it takes time before you say something. Your goal is to get used to speaking a foreign language, not to win a race.

Finally, you should organise conversation sessions and not use a dictionary. This way, you will learn how to handle unfamiliar words and prepare yourself for real-life conversation.

This was just one example of how you can slowly get out of your comfort zone.

You may want to use a different approach to improve your skills. This is fine, as long as you keep making things a bit harder for yourself.

To make progress in a foreign language, you should constantly challenge yourself. If you keep doing the things you are good at, it may be hard to advance.

ACTION PLAN

~Break your big goals into smaller ones.

~Try different learning resources and strategies and use the ones that work best for you.

~Reach out to other learners or native speakers to solve your doubts.

~Do different activities.

~Make the foreign language an important part of your life.

~Get out of your comfort zone.

CHECKPOINT

~You have chosen the best resources and strategies to learn a language ✔

~You do different activities and constantly get out of your comfort zone ✔

Great! Nothing can stop you now!

RECAP

~The best way to make progress without feeling overwhelmed is to break your big goals into smaller ones. Big goals can be intimidating and seem out of reach, while small ones can give you more confidence that you can do it.

~Try different learning strategies to find out what works best for you. This way, you will learn faster, and it will be easier to remember what you have learned.

~Stop assuming that whatever you are doing to learn a language is your best option. Whether you are new to foreign languages or have some experience on your side, get ready to question your method. It may open new doors for you.

~Choosing the appropriate learning resources is as important as selecting the strategies that work best for you. Search the Internet for tips and reviews to decide which ones to use.

~When you can't find the answer to your question on your own, you should post it on a language forum or discussion website. By connecting with other learners and native speakers, you will make sure that your doubts don't build up, and you can stay focused on your goal.

~A basic knowledge of grammar and vocabulary is enough to be able to read, watch a movie, speak and do many other things. Don't let the idea of 'not knowing enough' slow you down.

~Doing different activities will make the learning process exciting and stimulating. If you do the same things over and over again, you may lose interest and eventually quit.

~Make the foreign language an important part of your life. This will help you perceive it as 'something you don't want to do without'.

~Constantly get out of your comfort zone. If you keep doing the things you are good at, it may be hard to make progress.

CHAPTER THREE

FROM 'LET'S DO IT' TO 'I DID IT'!

One of the biggest challenges for language learners is to become fluent at speaking. Getting beyond a solid knowledge of grammar and vocabulary can be difficult; especially if the steps to follow are unclear.

In this chapter, we will explore how you can break the wall of words and rules and excel at conversation.

BECOMING FLUENT

Sometimes I feel like the word 'fluent' is the source of all problems for language learners. We tend to associate this word with 'sounding like' or 'having the same knowledge' as a native speaker, but is this what it means?

You are fluent when you can use a language **well** and **without difficulty**. Fluency has nothing to do with your accent or how many words you know.

As long as people understand you, you can keep your accent; it doesn't make you less fluent. And it doesn't matter if you don't know some words; what matters is your ability to get around them.

The more you use a language, the more you will come across unfamiliar words. The more you talk to people, the more likely they are to point out you have an accent. (At least, this is what happened to me.)

Instead of trying to 'sound like a native speaker' or learning as many words as they know, you should ask yourself: 'Can I communicate well? Can I express what I have in mind even if I don't know a word?'

The ability to overcome obstacles when they arise makes you more fluent than knowing a long list of words or having the perfect accent.

If you compare yourself to native speakers, you may waste your time chasing unnecessary skills. You may also try to become fluent in all areas of a language when it's not relevant to your goal.

For example, if you want to speak a language while travelling, you should prioritise conversation. You don't need to excel at reading and writing (unless you want to).

When you think about becoming fluent, forget about native speakers and focus on **your skills** and **how you want to use a language**. You will save time and energy and become fluent much faster.

FROM THE START

It is rare to find a learner who is not interested in speaking a foreign language. Usually, it is the moment we dream of the most; but for some reason, we tend to put it off.

Some learners believe they need to know grammar and vocabulary to perfection before they can talk. Others are too concerned with making mistakes.

By now, it should be clear that aiming for a perfect knowledge of words and rules can slow down your progress. As for mistakes, have you ever heard of anyone who has learned a language without making them?

The longer you wait before you start speaking, the harder it will be to learn. You can't expect to study grammar and vocabulary for months and then suddenly speak.

If you want to excel at conversation, it's better to approach it **gradually** and **as a beginner**.

You can go online right now and find someone to help you practise. All you have to do is exchange conversation lessons; that is to say, you offer conversation in your language in exchange for conversation in a foreign language.

If you prefer face-to-face sessions, you can post a message on advertisement websites like *Craigslist*[21] and *Gumtree.*[22] Simply include your native language and language of interest, your availability, and suggest a public place where you can meet (e.g. a cafe or your local library).

If you'd rather talk to someone online, you can use language exchange websites like

---

[21] http://www.craiglist.org
[22] https://www.gumtree.com/

Conversation Exchange,[23] *The Mixxer* [24] and *Speaky.*[25] This option is great for those on a busy schedule who want to skip commuting times.

By talking to a fluent or native speaker, you will make sure that what you say is correct. Most importantly, you will take your listening skills to the next level.

No matter how many videos, podcasts or movies you watch, it will never be the same as interacting with someone. Speaking is what will give you a better understanding and mastery of a language.

So what are you waiting for? It's time for conversation!

---

[23] https://www.conversationexchange.com/
On *Conversation Exchange*, you can also organise face-to-face conversation sessions.
[24] https://www.language-exchanges.org/
[25] https://www.speaky.com/

(Read on for some tips on how to approach your first conversation sessions with confidence.)

CHEAT SHEET

My first experience with conversation in a foreign language was as enjoyable as preparing my tax return. I did it because I had to, but I would have gladly done something else.

The issue was that I thought I had to start from scratch. I didn't want to put together a sentence while someone was waiting for me to say something; I just wanted to talk without feeling uncomfortable.

I wish I could tell you it's possible to speak flawlessly from the start, but I think it's rare. Instead, I'll share with you a strategy that will make your conversation sessions enjoyable and help you feel more confident when speaking.

This is the strategy I have used as a learner and as a teacher. In my experience, if you put it into practice, your skills will improve faster, and you will have a more positive experience while learning a language.

In this section, I will show you how 'conversation as a beginner' doesn't necessarily mean 'starting from scratch'.

So assuming you've just organised your first conversation session, what should you do next?

Instead of frantically reviewing vocabulary and grammar, my advice is to:

~Prepare a list of questions and answers likely to come up during the first sessions.

~Translate them into the foreign language.

~Use them as a reference during your sessions.

Don't worry, I did some of the work for you.

Below, I've included some of the most common questions and answers for early conversation sessions and a few sentences to discuss different topics. If you subscribe to my website,[26] I can send you a Word document of my sentences, which will make the next step easier.

How this strategy works:

~Copy and paste[27] all my sentences into Google Translate.[28]

~On the left side, select English.

---

[26] https://www.federicalupis.com/my-books. Follow the link and scroll down to the bottom of the page.
[27] If you are not familiar with this process, search on YouTube: 'How to copy and paste on laptop/computer'.
[28] https://translate.google.com/

~On the right side, select the language you want to learn.[29]

~Copy and paste the translation from Google Translate into my Word document, next to the English equivalent; e.g. learners of German will copy and paste 'Guten Tag!' next to 'Hello!'.

~Print the document and use it during your conversation sessions.

Please note that Google Translate may not be one hundred per cent accurate. To make sure your translations are correct, you have two options. You can ask your conversation partner/teacher to check them before your first session or correct your sentences as you use them. If possible, go with the first option so you

---

[29] At present, Google Translate offers translations in over one hundred languages. If the language you want to learn is not one of them, you can look for another online translation tool or use a dictionary.

will have more time to talk during your sessions.

The aim of this exercise is not to memorise sentences, but to have a support to lean on when you are just starting out conversation.

Believe me, answering a question, even if what you say isn't perfect, will give you more confidence and encourage you to do more. I have experienced it myself, and I have seen it with my students.

Now, let's cut to the chase. Here are my sentences:

First conversation sessions
Generic introduction and getting to know each other

~Hello! Pleased to meet you. My name is... What's your name?

~My name is... Nice to meet you too.

~How are you today?

~I'm well, and you?

~I'm fine thanks/I'm tired, please go easy on me!

~Where are you from?

~I'm from… And you?

~Where do you live?

~I live in…

~How old are you?

~I am… years old.

~What do you do for a living?

~I'm a student. I'm studying…

~I work as…

~I am retired.

~What would you like to do when you finish your studies?

~Tell me about a typical day at work.

~Do you have any hobbies?

~How long have you been learning...? – e.g. 'How long have you been learning Spanish?'

~I have been learning... for... months/years.

~Why do you want to learn...? – e.g. 'Why do you want to learn Spanish?'

~I want to learn... because/to... – e.g. 'I want to learn Spanish to surprise my grandparents. They are from Madrid.'

~Have you ever been to...? – e.g. 'Have you ever been to Cuba?'

~Yes, last year/... years ago.

~No, I haven't, but I'd like to go one day.

~What did you like most about…? – e.g. 'What did you like most about Cuba?'

~I loved…

~Did you like it?

~I liked it/No, I didn't.

~What's your favourite book/movie/song?

~My favourite book/movie/song is…

~What is the book/movie/song about?

~The book/movie/song is about…

~Who is your favourite actor/singer/author? What do you like about them?

~My favourite actor/singer/author is… I love the fact that…

~Can you cook?

~Yes, I can/No, I can't.

~What's your favourite food?

~My favourite food is…

~Do you like…? – e.g. 'Do you like pasta?'

~Yes, I love it/No, I don't.

~Do you prefer… or… – e.g. 'Do you prefer Thai or Vietnamese?'

~Do you play any sports?

~Yes, I play…/No, I don't.

~What sport do you like?

~I like…/I don't like any sports.

~Do you have any pets?

~Yes, I have a… His/her name is…/No, I don't have any pets.

~What do you like to do in your free time?

~I like…

~Tell me about your last holiday. Where did you go? Did you travel with someone or by yourself?

~My last holiday was in… I went with…/by myself.

~What did you do there?

~I visited... I had a great time!

~Would you rather… or…? – e.g. 'Would you rather be invisible or be able to read people's minds?'

~I'd rather be… – e.g. 'I'd rather be invisible'.

~What's on your bucket list?

~I'm sorry, I didn't understand. Can you repeat, please?

~Got it, thanks!

~Could you please talk slower?

~How do you say... in...? – e.g. 'How do you say *cheers!* in Italian?'

~What does... mean? – e.g. 'What does *salute!* mean?'

~It means... – e.g. 'It means *cheers!*'

~How do you spell that?

~What are your plans for the weekend?

~This weekend, I will...

~I have no plans for the weekend.

~OK, that's all for today. I'll see you next week.

~Thanks for your help! See you next week.

Following conversation sessions
Questions and answers to discuss
different topics

~What do you think about...? – e.g. 'What do you think about space tourism?'

~I think it's a good/bad idea.

~I think it's good news/a serious issue.

~Do you think it's important to…? – e.g. 'Do you think it's important to believe in yourself?'

~I think so/I don't think so.

~In my opinion, it's important/not important because…

~Do you think it's possible…? – e.g. 'Do you think it's possible to never lie?'

~It depends/It's possible.

~I think so/I don't think so.

~Do you agree with…? – e.g. 'Do you agree with gun control?'

~I agree with it/I disagree with it.

~What is the difference between... and...? – e.g. 'What is the difference between a good beer and a great one?'

~The difference is...

~Have you ever...? – e.g. 'Have you ever been skydiving?'

~Yes, I have/No, I haven't.

~Was... better in the past or now? – e.g. 'Was fashion better in the past or now?'

~It is better now because.../It was better in the past because...

~What are the advantages/benefits of...? – e.g. 'What are the advantages of working from home?'

~The advantages/benefits are...

~What are the disadvantages of...? – e.g. 'What are the disadvantages of working from home?'

~The disadvantages are…

~What is the best/worst thing about...? – e.g. 'What is the best/worst thing about renting a house?'

~The best/worst thing about… is…

~Who do you think is the greatest person in history?

~I think the greatest person in history is…

~What do you like most about… – e.g. 'What do you like most about your country?'

~What do you like least about...? – e.g. 'What do you like least about your country?'

~What makes a good...? – e.g. 'What makes a good friendship?'

~What can we do to... – e.g. 'What can we do to help the environment?'

~When you were a child/teenager, did you...? – e.g. 'When you were a child/teenager, did you watch cartoons?'

~Now that you are an adult, do you still...? – e.g. 'Now that you are an adult, do you still watch cartoons?'

~Who... the most? Kids or adults? – e.g. 'Who watches TV the most? Kids or adults?'

~Do you think... is for everyone or is aimed more at children/adolescents/adults? – e.g. 'Do you think the *Harry Potter* movies are for everyone or are they aimed more at children/adolescents/adults?'

~What would you do if...? – e.g. 'What would you do if you won a million dollars?'

~Do you prefer… or…? – e.g. 'Do you prefer to wake up early or sleep in?'

~Do you prefer… alone or with someone? – e.g. 'Do you prefer travelling alone or with someone?'

~If you could…, what would you do? – e.g. 'If you could fly, what would you do?'

~Have you ever heard of…? – e.g. 'Have you ever heard of the game *Dungeons & Dragons*?'

~Yes, I've heard of it/No, it's the first time I've heard of it.

~Did you know that… – e.g. 'Did you know that karate, skateboarding, baseball and surfing will be part of the next Olympic games?'

~What are the risks of…? – e.g. 'What are the risks of never taking a risk?'

Some tips

~Share this sheet with your conversation partner so they can refer to it during your first sessions.

~If you notice more recurring sentences, add them to your sheet.

~Always listen carefully to the other speaker. Most of the time, you can use some of their words in your answer.

A GAME CHANGER

When I first approached conversation in a foreign language, I thought it would be the hardest thing in the world. My idea of talking to someone could be summarised as follows:

~Listen to the other speaker and try to understand **every single thing** they say.

~Put together a sentence **from scratch**, e.g. find the right vocabulary and tenses to create a meaningful sentence.

As it turns out, I was wrong about both.

First of all, you don't need to catch every single word to understand the overall message – more on this in the next paragraph.

Second, if you want to make conversation easier, you can try to use some of the other speaker's words. You don't have to make as many decisions as you think in the space of a minute.

For example, as I faced my first conversations in English, I was terrified at the idea of choosing the wrong tense. Because of this, I spent minutes trying to decide and said nothing at all.

Things improved significantly as soon as I noticed that most of the time, I could use the same tense as the other speaker. For example:

~**Did** you go to the Foo Fighters concert? Yes, I **did**.

~**Have** you ever been to a Pink Floyd concert? Yes, I **have**.
(Or at least I wish!)

This realisation was a game changer. From that point on, creating a sentence just got a lot easier, and I started enjoying conversation more.

Some of you may think my suggestion is common sense, but in my experience, it isn't. Both as a student and as a teacher, I've noticed that most language learners think they have to do everything themselves when it comes to speaking.

The truth is, it doesn't have to be like that!

By paying attention to what the other speaker is saying, conversation can become easier.

Not convinced? Try this strategy! You will be surprised at how well it works.

IF IT'S TOO HARD, MAKE IT SIMPLE!

The video game *Overcooked* used to drive me insane. For those who have never heard of it, it's a cooperative game where each player controls a chef who needs to prepare different dishes under a time limit.

Chefs are awarded up to three stars for their efforts, but my partner and I never managed to get the maximum reward.

At first, I blamed the developers – sorry guys! The game was too hard, and it was impossible to get the third star. Then, a friend of mine told me she played *Overcooked* with her partner and got three stars in all levels.

How was this possible?! Did the developers make it easier for them? No way! There had to be a secret to getting the third star.

So I decided to watch people playing *Overcooked* on YouTube. And I immediately realised that, despite our best efforts, my partner and I were inefficient.

As soon as we changed our strategy, winning the third star became easier. Sometimes, we had to try a few times before we could get it, but we managed to finish the game with three stars in all levels.

When learning a language, you may feel the way I did when I couldn't get the result I wanted.

You may think the language is too hard and impossible to learn. You may even believe that other people have it easier for some mysterious reason.

My advice is to ignore these kinds of thoughts and try to 'beat the language' instead!

Start from successful learners. Can you get any advice from them? By searching the Internet, you will be able to read the stories of many people who have become fluent in the language you are learning. Use their experience to your advantage.

Then focus on what you find difficult and try to come up with a solution. For example, if you don't know a word in the foreign language, can you use a synonym? What about a definition?

Let's pretend you don't remember the word for 'pub' in the foreign language. You could say 'the place where people drink beer' instead. It doesn't matter if this isn't the definition you would find in the dictionary; as long as other people understand what you mean.

Eventually, you will have to learn the word for 'pub'. In the meantime, this strategy will help you keep talking when you don't know how to say something.

What if you find it difficult to understand other people in conversation?

My advice is to combine context with the words you can understand and see if you can guess. Let me explain.

Some learners are so focused on understanding every word that they end up sabotaging themselves. Unless they catch everything the other speaker is saying, they refrain from talking, assuming they won't be able to respond.

In many cases, however, context paired with a few words can help you guess. For example, if you have just met someone and can only understand 'where' 'you', they are probably asking where you're from.

Guessing isn't an excuse not to improve your listening skills. It is a way to gain more confidence in your abilities.

By using this strategy, you will realise that you can understand other people, even if you can't catch everything they say. And if your guess is wrong, you can always ask the other speaker to repeat and talk more slowly. It's not like you have anything to lose by trying.

These were just a few examples of how to get better at conversation. You can discover many more by talking to other learners or by checking out my book *Why you're not fluent and how to fix it*.

As I tell my students, there is always a way to make things easier. You just have to be patient and keep pushing when you find obstacles along the way.

Tip Go online and find a list of common words in the foreign language. For example, you could search for 'household items + your language of interest' – e.g. 'household items + Korean'. Choose a few words and try replacing them with a synonym or a definition, always in the foreign language.

With some practice, it will be easier to use this strategy in conversation.

LET IT GO

If I had to pick the main reasons why people don't become fluent, I would put self-doubt first and fear of making mistakes second. Self-doubt would come first, just because many learners quit before they even get to the stage of fear.

Ironically, the more you learn a language, the more you may be afraid of making mistakes. Since you know more, you have more options to choose from. So how can you be sure your choice is correct?

Whether you are in a class or a self-taught learner, fear tends to get worse when you start practising conversation. As you interact with someone, you want to show them you are good at the foreign language and you don't want to make mistakes.

In this respect, fear can be good. It can push you to do your best and improve. But if you let it take over, it may prevent you from becoming fluent.

Mistakes are part of learning. Nobody has ever mastered a language without making them.

If you say something wrong, you can correct it and learn. If you always use the same sentences, you may not go wrong, but it will be hard to improve.

Next time you worry about mistakes, pretend you have a friend who is learning your language. If they made a mistake, what would you think?

Absolutely nothing bad! On the contrary, you would encourage and admire them for their efforts.

You should have the same attitude towards yourself.

Learning a new language involves making mistakes. The sooner you accept this, the easier it will become to practise conversation.

Tip Accepting mistakes doesn't mean you want to keep making them.

If you want to improve, it's a good idea to start a list of words and sentences you often get wrong. You don't need to take note of every little thing; just the main ones.

From time to time, go through your list to refresh your memory. This strategy will help you learn from your mistakes and improve your skills.

Interesting fact Right after moving to London, I needed a new pair of headphones. So I went to a big shop in the city and looked around, but I couldn't find what I wanted.

Meanwhile, a young guy walked up to me and asked: 'Do you need any help?'

I paused for a few seconds and repeated my question in my head. Not making mistakes was of the utmost importance. Then I said: 'Yes, please. Do you have any handcuffs?'

The guy froze and blushed. I looked at him, clueless.

I was so caught up in my thoughts that my brain was overloaded.

'I'm sorry, but we don't sell any handcuffs here' he replied, embarrassed. At that point, I realised what I had said, and I wanted to disappear.

It was one of the most embarrassing moments of my life, but also one of the funniest memories. If I told you all the mistakes I made while using a foreign language, I could probably write another book.

We all make mistakes, and we all learn from them. But the most important thing is that looking back, we will have some pretty good memories!

IT DOES MATTER

Do you do more things for the people who encourage and support you, or for those who criticise you all the time?

I go above and beyond for the people who appreciate me. I stay away from the other category and do nothing for them unless I have to. It's probably not the best attitude, but that's just how I am.

Now apply the same principle to learning a language. Do you think it will be easier to become fluent if you keep criticising yourself or if you start appreciating your efforts?

Your attitude does matter. It matters more than anyone else's.

Be hard on yourself for your supposed failures and guess what? You will put yourself down, and it will be difficult to get the result you want.

Start noticing every little step forward and everything will change. You will feel encouraged to do more, and it will be easier to reach your goal.

After a Japanese session, I take a few minutes to appreciate what I have learned.

In the beginning, I only thought about my mistakes and how far I was from becoming fluent, and I was always feeling down. Since I focused on the positives, learning has become much more enjoyable, and I feel like I am progressing faster.

If you tend to be hard on yourself, shift your attention towards what you have achieved and acknowledge your efforts.

A simple change of perspective will make you feel more positive about learning and encourage you to do more to achieve your goal.

DON'T FALL INTO THE TRAP

Some learners do a great job. They do different activities and often practise conversation. They make learning a language a habit, and then… they fall into the trap of comparing their progress to someone else's.

'That guy learned how to speak in a couple of months. Why is it taking me so long?'

This kind of comparison is pointless; unless you talk to that learner and find out if they can help you improve.

Maybe they are using a strategy you are not aware of; maybe they have more time to practise. What if they know another language that is helping them learn faster?

Unless you find out, comparing your progress is just a way of setting yourself up for failure.

In your mind, you think you should be as good as someone else. If you are not, you may blame your lack of skills and convince yourself that you're not good at foreign languages.

I know because I did it myself.

I used to compare my progress to that of other learners on the Internet. When my results didn't match theirs, I used it as proof that I wasn't good enough to learn Japanese on my own.

Until one day, I realised I didn't even know those learners. What was their language background? What strategies were they using? I didn't know. So why were they so relevant to my progress?

Since then, I have decided to concentrate on what I can do to improve my language skills. I don't care if Mr So-and-So can speak Mandarin and read Arabic while walking on a tightrope – unless he can teach me how to do it!

If you want to become fluent in a language, you should focus on what **you** can do to reach your goal and bring someone else into the picture only if they can help you improve your skills.

This way, you will get rid of useless pressure and stay focused on your goal.

THE END RESULT

We all go through that moment when we feel like we're doing everything right, but the result we want isn't coming. 'I've been practising conversation for weeks, why am I not fluent yet?'

Having your goal clear in your mind is important, but if you focus too much on the end result, it can be counterproductive.

Whatever you are doing now will become an obstacle to your 'real objective', something that is holding you back. When, in fact, everything you do contributes to your progress.

A tedious grammar exercise may help you show off your language skills during your summer holiday. A difficult listening comprehension may help you make a great impression on the foreign committee visiting your company.

If you want to become fluent in a language, you should celebrate every little achievement without rushing to the end.

The learning process tends to be slow in the beginning; especially if it's the first time you learn a foreign language.

Things get easier with practice, but it's common to get to a point where your skills become stable, and you feel like you can't take the step to become fluent. I have been there, and like me, many other learners.

The essential thing is to keep going and never give up.

You can ask anyone who has become fluent in a language, and they will tell you it didn't happen in a flash. They advanced step by step until, at some point, they started making progress faster.

Maybe it will take you longer to get the same results as another person, but you could improve a lot more after that point.

Everything you are learning is taking you one step closer to your objective. You just have to be persistent and focus on your achievements rather than how far you are from your goal.

AND FINALLY

Some learners feel like they have to do something extraordinary to learn a language. 'If I could move there for six months, I'm sure I would become fluent!' 'If I had the money to buy that expensive course, I would improve much faster.'

The truth is, these sorts of things can help, but they are not crucial to your success.

You may move to another country, but stick with people who speak your native language, and learn very little. You may also spend tons of money on the best resources, and still not achieve the results you want.

What makes all the difference is **your approach to learning**.

Goals become a reality once you turn them into a habit, and your progress depends on how willing you are to get out of your comfort zone.

Once you make a language part of your routine, it will be much harder to quit. And if you keep challenging yourself, you will keep improving. There's no way that you will stay the same.

I cannot stress enough the importance of your attitude when learning a language. You should praise yourself for your hard work and commitment and never bring yourself down.

If you can focus on every little success, rather than how much work is left to do, it will be easier to advance and reach your goal.

I hope this book will help you commit to learning a language and confidently face any obstacles you may find along the way.

As someone who went from struggling with languages to making a career out of them, I am convinced that you can learn any language you want! You just need to give more structure to the learning process.

If you:

~Make learning a language a habit.
~Use the learning strategies that work best for you.
~Constantly get out of your comfort zone.
~Have a positive attitude towards mistakes.
~Practise conversation from the start and do different activities.
~Get the feedback of a fluent or native speaker on your progress.

I am sure you will become **fluent on the first try**!

If you wish to continue with me, I would love to take you through my strategies to learn the pronunciation, grammar, vocabulary of any language, and a detailed list of conversation exercises in my book *Why you're not fluent and how to fix it.*[30]

I hope to see you there!

Fin

---

[30] *Why you're not fluent and how to fix it* is available on all Amazon marketplaces in the e-book and paperback format. You can find the link to your Amazon marketplace on my website https://www.federicalupis.com/my-books.

ACTION PLAN

~Approach conversation gradually and as a beginner.

~Focus on your skills and how you want to use the language.

~Accept mistakes as part of learning.

~Don't compare yourself to other learners unless they can help you improve.

~Celebrate your achievements and never give up! By now, you have all the tools you need to become fluent!

CHECKPOINT

~You are committed to learning a language ✔

~You know how to keep learning and avoid the risk of giving up halfway ✔

~You are using all the strategies that will help you become fluent ✔

Great job! You have come such a long way!

RECAP

~You are fluent when you can use a language well and without difficulty. Fluency has nothing to do with 'sounding like' or 'having the same knowledge' as a native speaker.

~You can't expect to study grammar and vocabulary for months and then suddenly speak. You should approach conversation gradually and as a beginner.

~At any point in the learning process, you may think the language is too hard, and it is impossible to learn. You may even believe that other people have it easier for some mysterious reason. Ignore these sorts of thoughts; there is always a way to make the learning process easier.

~Nobody has ever learned a language without making mistakes. If you say something wrong, you can correct it and learn. If you always use the same sentences, you may not go wrong, but it will be hard to improve.

~If you ever doubt yourself and think you'll never reach your goal, move your attention towards what you have already achieved. A simple change of perspective will make it easier to advance.

~Bring other learners into the picture only if they can help you improve your skills.

~Don't rush towards the end. Everything you are learning is taking you one step closer to your goal.

~If you make learning a language a habit, constantly get out of your comfort zone, and practise conversation from the start, you will become fluent on the first try!

BOOK OVERVIEW

Reading this book is just the beginning of your journey to master a language. During the learning process, you'll probably need to go back to some paragraphs or chapters to refresh your memory.

Below, I've included a quick summary of this book to help you find the information you need faster.

CHAPTER ONE

To successfully learn a foreign language, you need to:

~**Know your goal**. (Why are you learning a foreign language?)

~**Set a realistic time frame**. (By considering your approach to learning and other learners' experience.)

~Make learning a language a habit. (Plan your week ahead, or set aside ten minutes a day to learn a language.)

~Find the motivation to learn a language. (What can motivate you to do more?)

~Put together a simple plan and keep it with you when you are studying. Being reminded of what you want and how you want to achieve it will help you commit to learning a language more.

CHAPTER TWO

Once a language is part of your routine, it will be harder to quit, but not impossible. Other factors can take you away from your goal in the long term.

To keep making progress, it is essential that you:

~Break your big goals into smaller ones.

~Use the **strategies that work best for you**.

~Choose **effective learning resources**.

~**Reach out to other learners** so that your doubts don't build up.

~**Do different activities** to keep the learning process exciting and stimulating.

~Make a language an **important part of your life**.

~Constantly **get out of your comfort zone**. If you keep doing the things you are good at, it may be hard to make progress.

CHAPTER THREE

~You are **fluent** when you can **use a language well and without difficulty**. Fluency has nothing to do with your accent or how many words you know.

~You should **practise conversation from the start** and get the feedback of a fluent or native speaker to check your progress.

~**Accept mistakes** as part of learning.

~**Don't compare yourself to other learners** unless they can help you improve.

~**Focus on every small success** rather than how much work is left to do. This way, it will be easier to advance and reach your goal.

If you:

~**Make learning a language a habit**.

~Use **the learning strategies that work best** for you.

~Constantly **get out of your comfort zone**.

~Have a **positive attitude towards mistakes**.

~**Practise conversation from the start** and do different activities.

~**Get** the **feedback** of a fluent or native speaker on your progress.

You will become **fluent on the first try**!

I'D LOVE TO HEAR FROM YOU!

What do you think of *Fluent on the first try*?

Thank you for reading this book! I hope you enjoyed it and that my advice will help you achieve your goal.

Now I'd love to hear from you!

If you found this book useful, **I would be grateful if you could post a short review on Amazon.**[31]

Your support really makes a difference.

Thank you!

I wish you all the best.

Federica

---

[31] You can find the link to your Amazon marketplace on my website https://www.federicalupis.com/my-books.

ACKNOWLEDGEMENTS

I'd like to start by thanking my family: my mum Vera, my dad Rocco and my sister Valentina. You are my strength and my inspiration, and I can't wait for the moment when I can hug you again. Keep the wine ready because it's going to be a hell of a celebration!

Thank you to my 'partner in mischief' Ash. Sharing my life with you is an incredible adventure. I couldn't have done this without your love and support. I'm looking forward to more anime, more dumplings, and more 'nonsense just because it's fun'.

A big thank you to my friend Michael. You are always there for me and keep my mood high. As you said: 'Yesterday is not an option'. I agree, but remember that any day is a good day to share a great meal and wine!

Thanks to the friends of a lifetime: Vanessa, Elisa, Antonia, Veronica, Diego, La Senior, Sandra, Elena, Davidino, Francesca, Rosalba, Gianca and Crest. I cherish our memories together, and I can't wait to make new ones. I love you guys!

A big shout out to: Zia Frenga, Fabiano, Franca, Massimo S., Massimo P., Cristina, Oksana, Jack and Enya. You have a special place in my heart.

Thank you to all my students. When I'm with you, I feel like I'm with family. I'm lucky to have you in my life.

And finally, thanks to all my readers. It is a privilege to be able to share my passion with you. I hope I helped you reach your goal of becoming fluent!

ABOUT THE AUTHOR

Federica Lupis is a language professional with a passion for motivating people and helping them achieve their goals.

After gaining her master's degree with honours in foreign languages, she qualified as an interpreter and translator in Australia, where she currently lives.

Federica has over 10 years of experience teaching languages, and she has no doubt that with her method, anyone can become fluent in any language.

In her first book *Why you're not fluent and how to fix it*, she revealed the best strategies to learn any language. Now, she has focused on the secrets to keep learning until you get the results you want.

To stay current of Federica's upcoming books, visit https://www.federicalupis.com/.

OTHER BOOKS FROM THE SAME AUTHOR

Why you're not fluent and how to fix it

LEARN ANY LANGUAGE YOU WANT ONCE AND FOR ALL.

Stop thinking that you don't have a talent for languages and **stop blaming your memory**.

If you want to know what's really keeping you from becoming fluent, this book has the answer – and the solution.

From pronunciation to vocabulary, grammar and conversation, Federica Lupis will reveal the best strategies to learn and **master any language**. She won't just give you a list of ideas; she will help you develop an **easy plan to reach your goal**.

With a friendly tone and constant encouragement, you will discover the strategies that work best for you, and you will **learn faster**. More importantly, you will become **fluent at speaking**, as well as reading and writing.

Federica is fluent in four languages and has **over 10 years of experience** helping people become fluent. She has both formal education and the knowledge of a self-taught learner.

Follow the advice in this book and **you will learn any language you want once and for all**!

To purchase my book, visit my website https://www.federicalupis.com/my-books.
Thank you!

EDITORIAL WORK

Kyara and the Ancestors' Ring

By Saveria Parisi

Italian edition

English edition out early 2021.

Please see my website
https://www.federicalupis.com/editorial-work.

Your new journey into a world of adventure, mystery and magic...

Kyara, a brave and curious girl, is intrigued by the discovery of a **secret passage** and **a ring with extraordinary powers**.

The old mansion where she lives, immersed in the wonderful land of Sicily, is the scene of **inexplicable events** that prompt her to investigate her mysterious family.

With her inseparable friends, Kyara will experience moments beyond logic and full of **suspense**, as she combines the **clues** she finds along the way…

Will our **brave heroine** be able to solve an **intricate puzzle** and defeat a **powerful enemy**?

It's up to you to find out!

Printed in Great Britain
by Amazon

47373244R00098